FAITH CHAT WITH PRW

Quiet Meditation Moments

Volume 1

PHYLLIS R. WELCH

GWW
PUBLISHING CO.

Faith Chat With PRW: Quiet Meditation Moments, Volume 1

Email requests info@gwwpublishing.com

Ordering Information:
Quantity sales. Special discounts are available on quantity purchases by corporations, associations, and others. For details, contact the publisher at the email address above.

Orders by trade bookstores and wholesalers. Please contact publisher at email address above.

GWW Publishing
PO Box 291764
Columbia, SC 29229
www.greaterwomen.com/publishing

Printed in USA

First Printing, 2017

ISBN-13: 978-0-9991975-3-0

DEDICATION

This book is dedicated to everyone known and unknown who has helped me to grow spiritually. To all those who have prayed for me fervently and to all those who have encouraged me along the way.

I would especially like to thank my sister and dear friend Elder Jacqueline Knight who continuously encourages me to remain steadfast and unmovable. I thank God for the gift he gave me whom I call Mother, Louise Walker, who had the faith to trust God with all three of her children. A woman of great strength who raised us in the church and imparted into us the gift of Jesus! Thank you, Mom, I love you! I would like to thank Elder Chantae Williams who obeyed God to answer His call in her life to help so many of us to exit our comfort zones and use the gifts that God gave us to become authors.

Finally, I don't have enough words or praise to express my heart to God our Father for choosing me to serve Him! I am grateful for every gift and every opportunity He affords me to share what He has imparted to me. It is my prayer that every person who will read this book will experience a divine moment in His presence!

TABLE OF CONTENTS

INTRODUCTION

The Holy Spirit often nudges us to write down little nuggets from our personal moments of meditation and we ignore Him. If we would only listen, we would find that there was purpose in the nudging. This book is not written to give spiritual advice, council, or guidance. It is merely a glimpse into my personal time with God.

Just my personal reflections while meditating on God's Word. It is my prayer that you will find something that will encourage you, edify you, and lift you up. It is just a peep into the window of my "faith chats" with the Lord.

I pray the blessings of the Lord upon every reader.

God Bless,

Elder Phyllis R. Welch

HAVE YOU HAD YOUR FAITH CHAT TODAY?

DAY 1

Romans 4:20-21

"He staggered not at the promise of God through unbelief; but was strong in faith, giving glory to God; And being fully persuaded that, what he had promised, he was able also to perform."
(KJV)

Dear Father in heaven,

It's a beautiful day. Thank you again for another chance to bless your name. Thank you for the example of Abraham's faith. He staggered not at your promise through unbelief, but was strong in faith. Holy Spirit strengthen our faith as we give glory to God. Help us be fully persuaded and know that what God has promised us He is still able to perform.

"Loving you forever, Lord Jesus and I excitedly wait to sup with you again!"

DAY 2

ISAIAH 26:3-4

"Thou wilt keep him in perfect peace, whose mind is stayed on thee: because he trusteth in thee. Trust ye in the Lord for ever: for in the LORD JEHOVAH is everlasting strength."
(KJV)

Dear Father in heaven,

Thank you for working all things together for our good. Thank you for keeping us in perfect peace as we stay our minds on you. We trust you and there is no doubt about it. Saints I admonish you to trust him forever. He is the Lord God Jehovah and his strength is everlasting.

"Loving you forever, Lord Jesus and I excitedly wait to sup with you again!"

DAY 3

MATTHEW 12:13

"Then saith he to the man, Stretch forth thine hand. And he stretched it forth; and it was restored whole, like as the other." (KJV)

Dear Father in heaven,

Thank you for restoration. Just as Jesus healed the man with the withered hand, remind us too that if we would stretch forth the withered dried up things in our lives. You still restore lives, relationships, and situations.

"Loving you forever, Lord Jesus and I excitedly wait to sup with you again!"

DAY 4

DEUTERONOMY 6:11-12

"And the house full of all good things, which thou filledst not, and wells digged, which thou diggedst not, vineyards and olive trees, which thou plantedst not; when thou shalt have eaten and be full; Then beware lest thou forget the Lord, which brought thee forth out of the land of Egypt, from the house of bondage." (KJV)

Dear Father in heaven,

Thank you for being mindful of us. Thank you for increase. You have blessed us beyond all that we could imagine or think. This morning I appreciate this word. You told the Israelites to stay alert and to beware and not forget when they came into their wealthy place not to forget how you brought them out of the house of bondage. Help us to remember how you have also brought us out of the house of bondage so we won't become so comfortable and full that we just focus on the provisions that we forget the one who made the provisions. Help us not to return to our old traditions and our old routines. Help us to remember how you have delivered us.

"Loving you forever, Lord Jesus and I excitedly wait to sup with you again."

DAY 5

Matthew 5:13

"Ye are the salt of the earth; but if the salt have lost his savour, wherewith shall it be salted? It is thenceforth good for nothing, but to be cast out, and to be trodden under foot of men." (KJV)

Dear Father in heaven,

Thank you for calling us and giving purpose to our lives. Jesus said: "We are the salt of the earth." Salt is used to season or to preserve and add flavor. It has a distinctive quality and is easily recognized. Lord help us to season the lives of those we encounter with your word. Holy Spirit help us to remember we do have a distinctive quality and it's not because of who we are, but it's because we belong to God.

"Loving you forever, Lord Jesus and I excitedly wait to sup with you again!"

DAY 6

Proverbs 14:26-27

"In the fear of the Lord is strong confidence: and his children shall have a place of refuge. The fear of the Lord is a fountain of life, to depart from the snares of death." (KJV)

Dear Father in heaven,

Thank you for being our refuge and fountain of life! Our strong confidence is the result of our love, reverence, and obedience to and for you. The fear of the Lord has provided a way for us to depart from the snares of death. Therefore, we rejoice and give all glory to you O God for what you have imparted in us. Thank you for making us the beneficiaries of your inheritance.

"Loving you forever, Lord Jesus and I excitedly wait to sup with you again!"

DAY 7

John 15:7

"If ye abide in me, and my words abide in you, ye shall ask what ye will, and it shall be done unto you." (KJV)

Dear Father in heaven,

You are GREAT! No one can compare to you. Thank you Jesus for this word this morning; abide. To stay; to dwell; to hang around; to remain; to tarry or to live. If we stay and live in you and your word dwell and remain in us; we can ask what we will and it shall be done unto us. Help us Father to abide in the Word and in Christ Jesus. Let us ask according to your will and in agreement with your Word.

"Loving you forever, Lord Jesus and I excitedly wait to sup with you again!"

DAY 8

Psalm 130:5

"I wait for the Lord, my soul doth wait, and in his word do I hope." (KJV)

Dear Father in heaven,

I appreciate you! Thank you for teaching us how to wait on You. Regardless of the excitement we feel from knowing you are going to answer; we will wait on you. Our soul will wait. We wait because our hope rest in your Word. You cannot lie so we will wait. While we are waiting, we will thank You and praise You.

We wait:

W- Witness

A - Accept Your will

I - Invest in others spiritually

T - Testify of Your goodness.

"Loving you forever, Lord Jesus and I excitedly wait to sup with you again!"

DAY 9

PSALM 103:1-5

"Bless the lord, O my soul: and all that is within me, bless his holy name. Bless the Lord, O my soul, and forget not all his benefits: Who forgiveth all thine iniquities; who healeth all thy diseases; Who redeemeth thy life from destruction; who crowneth thee with lovingkindness and tender mercies; Who satisfieth thy mouth with good things; so that thy youth is renewed like the eagle's. (KJV)

Dear Father in heaven,

Loving You is splendid! So often, we rely on our insurance policies to protect our earthly possessions and have great confidence in the companies we have chosen, but we struggle with having great confidence in You. Remind us God of the benefits that no earthly entity can compare to or provide. You forgive all our sins. You heal all our diseases. You redeem our lives from destruction. You crown us with loving kindness and tender mercies. You satisfy our mouths with good things and our youth is renewed. Thank You for covering us!

"Loving you forever, Lord Jesus and I excitedly wait to sup with you again!"

DAY 10

PSALM 28:7-8

"The Lord is my strength and my shield; my heart trusted in him, and I am helped: therefore my heart greatly rejoiceth; and with my song will I praise him. The Lord is their strength, and he is the saving strength of his anointed." (KJV)

Dear Father in heaven,

Thank you for brand new mercies today. Thank You for protecting and defending me. I am not helpless because I know for sure that the Holy Spirit is my help. My heart rejoices in You and my soul makes her boast in You. Thank you for a holy passion to serve You. It's such an honour to me!

"Loving you forever, Lord Jesus and I excitedly wait to sup with you again!"

DAY 11

ACTS 3:6-10

"Then Peter said, Silver and gold have I none; but such as I have give I thee: In the name of Jesus Christ of Nazareth rise up and walk. And he took him by the right hand, and lifted him up: and immediately his feet and ankle bones received strength. And he leaping up stood, and walked and entered with them into the temple, walking, and leaping and praising God. And all the people saw him walking and praising God: And they knew that it was he which sat for alms at the Beautiful gate of the temple: and they were filled with wonder and amazement at that which had happened unto him." (KJV)

Dear Father in heaven,

You are all that we need. So many times, we may feel like we have nothing to offer those who are in need, but look a little closer. As believers, we have everything we need; Jesus Christ! If we would give them Jesus, He will change circumstances. Just remember where you were before in your life without Him and compare it to where you are now. Isn't it a wonder? Simply amazing? Yes, it is to you and everyone who knew you. Praise God! We are who we are by the grace of God! Give others who you have; Jesus Christ!

"Loving you forever, Lord Jesus and I excitedly wait to sup with you again!"

DAY 12

PSALM 34:8-9

"O taste and see that the Lord is good: blessed is the man that trusteth in him. O fear the Lord, ye his saints: for there is no want to them that fear him." (KJV)

Dear Father in heaven,

It's Friday and thank You for allowing grace and mercy to follow us all week long. We don't take this blessing for granted. Thank You for Your divine favor and provision. Thank You for seating us in heavenly places. O Lord, we have tasted and we have seen that you are so good. We are blessed because we trust You. If we fear You; reverence You and obey You we will want for absolutely nothing. What do you have a taste for?

"Loving you forever, Lord Jesus and I excitedly wait to sup with you again!"

DAY 13

PSALM 92 (1-15)

Dear Father in heaven,

You are good! Giving thanks unto the Lord is a very good thing. Lord You show us your loving kindness in the morning and your faithfulness every night. It's You who have made us glad through Your work. We agree that Your works are great and Your thoughts are very deep. You anoint us with fresh oil. Thank you for planting us in Your house and causing us to flourish. Yes, giving thanks unto the Lord is a very good thing.

"Loving you forever, Lord Jesus and I excitedly wait to sup with you again!"

DAY 14

DEUTERONOMY 10:12

"And now, Israel, what doth the Lord thy God require of thee, but to fear the Lord thy God, to walk in all his ways, and to love him, and to serve the Lord thy God with all thy heart and with all thy soul." (KJV)

Dear Father in heaven,

Thank You for a new day! A new opportunity to tell of your goodness. When I was lost in my sins I use to think that God was asking me to give up too much fun, but I didn't know that His joy was so much better than my fun. Now I know that what He requires is not hard at all because I love Him so! He requires us to fear Him; walk in all His ways; love Him; and to serve Him with all our hearts and souls. Thank You Father for teaching us how to circumcise our hearts.

"Loving you forever, Lord Jesus and I excitedly wait to sup with you again!"

DAY 15

JOHN 9:31

"Now we know that God heareth not sinners: but if any man be a worshipper of God, and doeth his will, him he heareth." (KJV)

Dear Father in heaven,

You are so gracious to us! There is such great joy that comes with knowing You. One of the benefits of worshipping You and doing Your will is a guarantee that You hear us when we call upon You. Thank you, Jesus for reconciling us back to the Father. We no longer have to ask the question: "Did God really hear our prayer?" No Saints of God, He doesn't put us on mute and He doesn't ignore or place a block on our calls. The old Saints use to sing: "The line is never busy."

"Loving you forever, Lord Jesus and I excitedly wait to sup with you again!"

DAY 16

3 JOHN 1:2

"Beloved, I wish above all things that thou mayest prosper and be in health, even as thy soul prospereth." (KJV)

Dear Father in heaven,

Thank You for the gift of the Holy Spirit who empowers us to do Your will! Your Word says that life and death are in the power of the tongue. Since this is true Saints, let us speak this blessing over those we love daily. The blessing that they would prosper and be in good health even as their souls prosper. Then Father use us to lead them to Christ, use us to show them Your love so their souls can prosper.

"Loving you forever, Lord Jesus and I excitedly wait to sup with you again!"

DAY 17

MATTHEW 9:27-29

"And when Jesus departed thence, two blind men followed him, crying, and saying, Thou Son of David, have mercy on us. And when he was come into the house, the blind men came to him: and Jesus saith unto them, Believe ye that I am able to do this? They said unto him, Yea, Lord."
(KJV)

Dear Father in heaven,

Thank You for strength! Strength to endure and persevere. I realize Jesus healed two blind men physically in this passage of scripture. My thoughts this morning: When the spiritually blind come into the house, (whether at church, home, work, or wherever believers may be) let it be known that Jesus is in the house! So that the blind can come to Him. Father let us ask the same question: "Do you believe Jesus can do this?" Father help them say yes, Lord Jesus touch them, and let it be done unto them according to their faith.

"Loving you forever, Lord Jesus and I excitedly wait to sup with you again!"

DAY 18

PSALM 145:1-2

"I will extol thee, my God, O king; and I will bless thy name for ever and ever. Everyday will I bless thee; and I will praise thy name for ever and ever." (KJV)

Dear Father in heaven,

Thank You again for the gift of life. For it's in You that we really live, move, and have our being. Thank You for sending Jesus "STRAIGHT OUTTA HEAVEN!" This morning Father I extol You; glorify, bless, and celebrate You. You are our God and King and every day I will bless Your holy name. There is no one I speak more highly of than You. Help us to give You the glory in everything we do.

"Loving you forever, Lord Jesus and I excitedly wait to sup with you again!"

DAY 19

JOHN 8:36

"If the Son therefore shall make you free, ye shall be free indeed." (KJV)

Dear Father in heaven,

Thank You for bringing us through. Thank You for Jesus Your only begotten Son who abideth in the house forever. Thank You that He has set us free indeed. Indeed: Unquestionably free; undeniably free; undoubtedly free indeed. So, help us to know that no one can hold us hostage to our past because Jesus has set us free in deed. Our deeds: We have been set free from the things we use to do!

"Loving you forever, Lord Jesus and I excitedly wait to sup with you again!"

DAY 20

"Love Note"

Lord Jesus, I just want to say to You today thank You for Your goodness and Your mercy. I realize I did absolutely nothing to deserve it. As I start my day I want You to know I love and appreciate You.

"Loving you forever, Lord Jesus and I excitedly wait to sup with you again!"

DAY 21

JEREMIAH 7:2

"Stand in the gate of the Lord's house, and proclaim there this word, and say, Hear the word of the lord, all ye of Judah, that enter in at these gates to worship the Lord." (KJV)

Dear Father in heaven,

Thank You for all those who have stood and continue to stand in the gate of Your house proclaiming Your Word. Remind us again that when we enter to worship we enter to hear the Word of the Lord. Thank You Father for the desire and privilege to hear Your Word.

"Loving you forever, Lord Jesus and I excitedly wait to sup with you again!"

DAY 22

"Thank You Note"

Dear Father in heaven,

Thank You for the men and women of God in my life who have planted and watered the seed, but I give You all the glory for the increase in my life.

"Loving you forever, Lord Jesus and I excitedly wait to sup with you again!"

DAY 23

MATTHEW 19:14-15

"But Jesus said, Suffer little children, and forbid them not, to come unto me: for of such is the kingdom of heaven. And he laid his hands on them, and departed thence." (KJV)

Dear Heavenly Father,

Thank You for blessing us and trusting us to raise and love our children because we know they are a blessing from You. Help us to realize that the best gift we can give them is to present and introduce them to Jesus Christ; Him crucified, resurrected from the dead, and alive forevermore! Holy Spirit empower us with the desire to teach them the Word of God.

"Loving you forever, Lord Jesus and I excitedly wait to sup with you again!"

DAY 24

ROMANS 8:38-39

"For I am persuaded, that neither death, nor life, nor angels, nor principalities, nor powers, nor things present, nor things to come, nor height, nor depth, nor any other creature, shall be able to separate us from the love of God, which is in Christ Jesus our Lord." (KJV)

Dear Father in heaven,

I am persuaded, convinced, and determined that NOTHING shall separate me from the love of God as long as I live a holy, consecrated and surrendered life unto Him. Can you say: "NOTHING?"

"Loving you forever, Lord Jesus and I excitedly wait to sup with you again!"

DAY 25

ROMAN 6:13

"Neither yield ye your members as instruments of unrighteousness unto sin: but yield yourselves unto God, as those that are alive from the dead, and your members as instruments of righteousness unto God." (KJV)

Dear Father in heaven,

I thank You for the tools and instructions You have given to the believers to live victoriously. Holy Spirit I ask You to empower us so that we will learn not to yield. Help us not to concede, surrender, not to be influenced, dissuaded, or to give up our rights over to the works of the enemy. Remind us continuously that we are indeed more than conquerors through Jesus Christ our Lord.

"Loving you forever, Lord Jesus and I excitedly wait to sup with you again!"

DAY 26

1 PETER 4:17

"For the time is come that judgment must begin at the house of God: and if it first begin at us, what shall the end be of them that obey not the gospel of God?" (KJV)

"THE DOORS OF THE CHURCH ARE OPEN"

"Loving you forever, Lord Jesus and I excitedly wait to sup with you again!"

DAY 27

JOHN 11:10:43

"And when he thus had spoken, he cried with a loud voice, Lazarus, come forth." (KJV)

Dear Father in heaven,

This morning I thank You for life. Thank You for bringing light into my darkness. Just as You called Lazarus from death, remind us that You have also called us to come forth. Remind us Lord Jesus that You have removed every stone that has hindered, blocked, and sealed us from answering Your call. Holy Spirit anoint us to be a witness to Your resurrection power to still raise the dead. You still have the power to save and raise those who are dead spiritually. Use us for Your glory!

"Loving you forever, Lord Jesus and I excitedly wait to sup with you again!"

DAY 28

MATTHEW 4:1:10

"Then saith Jesus unto him, Get thee hence, Satan: for it is written, Thou shalt worship the Lord thy God, and him only shalt thou serve."
(KJV)

Dear Father in heaven,

Again, I must say I am grateful to you! Thank You for the gift of Your precious and only Son Jesus Christ! Your love is unmeasurable, Your loving kindness is better than life. Holy Spirit thank You for showing me that the devil is always ready to bring temptation in three areas of my life spiritually. My appetite for Your Word, Your divine purpose for my life, and my worship. Help me to declare just as Jesus did: "It is written!" I want to live by Your Word, never abort Your purpose for me, and worship You only.

"Loving you forever, Lord Jesus and I excitedly wait to sup with you again!"

DAY 29

PHILIPPIANS 4:8

"Finally, brethren, whatsoever things are true, whatsoever things are honest, whatsoever things are just, whatsoever things are pure, whatsoever things are lovely, whatsoever things are of good report; if there be any virtue, and if there be any praise, think on these things." (KJV)

Dear Father in heaven,

I smile because You told me that Your thoughts are always turned toward me, which means I never have to wonder if anyone is thinking about me. So as a result of knowing this, I desire to think on whatsoever things are honest, just, lovely, pure, and of good report. I choose to think on these things. My thought life is important to You. So, I choose to let this mind be in me which was also in Christ Jesus!

"Loving you forever, Lord Jesus and I excitedly wait to sup with you again!"

DAY 30

LUKE 10:34

"And went to him, and bound up his wounds, pouring in oil and wine, and set him on his own beast, and brought him to an inn, and took care of him." (KJV)

Dear Father in heaven,

Thank You for brand new mercies! Your love is simply amazing! Holy Spirit I ask You today to lead and guide me into all truth. Help me to recognize every opportunity You bring my way to bind up the wounds of others. It may require some of my time, it may require me to give up my place of comfort, and it may even cost me money, but if it will point a soul to Jesus so be it.

"Loving you forever, Lord Jesus and I excitedly wait to sup with you again!"

DAY 31

"Love Note"

Dear Father in heaven,

I am elated that I have a relationship with You. It is the most rewarding, satisfying, everlasting, and precious relationship I have ever been blessed to have in my life. I love being in Your presence. I love talking with You and listening to You, but most of all I am excited just to obey You. Thank You for teaching me how to worship and love You better!

"Loving you forever, Lord Jesus and I excitedly wait to sup with you again!"

DAY 32

ECCLESIASTES 3:1

***"To everything there is a season, and a time to
every purpose under the heaven." (KJV)***

Dear Father in heaven,

I love You! Thank You for the time to fulfill my
purpose. Thank You for the time to birth forth what
You have placed inside of me. Thank You for my
harvest. Thank You for the time to build. Thank You
for my time of joy and dancing. Thank You for the
time to embrace Your promises. Thank You for the
power to refrain from embracing doubt and unbelief.
Thank You for the time to get and keep all that You
have promised to me. Thank You for the time to sit
quietly in Your presence and the time to speak to You
in prayer. Thank You for the time to fight for what is
right. I agree that the blessings of the Lord are rich
and add no sorrow.

"Loving you forever, Lord Jesus and I excitedly wait
to sup with you again!"

DAY 33

Exodus 12:23

"For the Lord will pass through to smite the Egyptians; and when he seeth the blood upon the lintel, and on the two side posts, the Lord will pass over the door, and will not suffer the destroyer to come in unto your houses to smite you." (KJV)

Dear Father in heaven,

As I sit to express my gratitude to you. Just like the children of Israel were instructed to apply the blood to the doorpost, I thank Jesus for applying His blood to the doorpost of my heart. Have you ever reflected upon your personal Passover meal? All the issues that were on your table when the blood of Jesus washed away your sins? Father thank You for allowing the death angel to pass by me.

"Loving you forever, Lord Jesus and I excitedly wait to sup with you again!"

DAY 34

I Thessalonians 2:4

"But as we were allowed of God to be put in trust with the gospel, even so we speak; not as pleasing men, but God, which trieth our hearts."

Dear Father in heaven,

Thank you for giving us the privilege of being allowed to be put in trust of the gospel! WOW! Help us to remember what an honor it is to represent You. Remind us that You didn't trust us with Your Word to speak to please men, but we speak to please You because it is You who trieth our hearts.

"Loving you forever, Lord Jesus and I excitedly wait to sup with you again!"

DAY 35

Psalm 1:3

"And he shall be like a tree planted by the rivers of water, that bringeth forth his fruit in his season; his leaf also shall not wither, and whatsoever he doeth shall prosper."

Dear Father in heaven,

Thank you for your law because it has brought so much fruit into my life. It has refreshed me, sustained me and most of all caused me to prosper in everything You have placed in my hands to do.

"Loving you forever, Lord Jesus and I excitedly wait to sup with you again!"

DAY 36

Psalm 100:4

"Enter into his gates with thanksgiving, and into his courts with praise: be thankful unto him, and bless his name."

Dear Father in heaven,

It's worship time! Let us not forget how we are instructed to enter. We are instructed to enter his gates with thanksgiving and into his courts with praise. Be thankful unto him and bless his name! It's worship time!

"Loving you forever, Lord Jesus and I excitedly wait to sup with you again!"

DAY 37

II Chronicles 7:1-3

"Now when Solomon had made an end of praying, the fire came down from heaven, and consumed the burnt offering and the sacrifices; and the glory of the lord filled the house. And the priests could not enter into the house of the Lord, because the glory of the Lord had filled the Lord's house. And when all the children of Israel saw how the fire came down, and the glory of the Lord upon the house, they bowed themselves with their faces to the ground upon the pavement, and worshipped, and praised the Lord, saying, For he is good; for his mercy endureth for ever."

Dear Father in heaven,

I simply want to say thank You this morning for You do all things well. Thank you for this passage of scripture. Father allow us to have the same experience when we pray in our churches and homes. May Your fire fall and consume us as we offer You our sacrifice of praise and present our bodies as living sacrifices unto You, holy and acceptable unto You. Holy Spirit consume us until our only response is to bow down in worship and praise Your name. Let Your glory and Your presence totally consume us. Let us continue to speak that You are good and Your mercy endureth forever.

"Loving you forever, Lord Jesus and I excitedly wait to sup with you again!"

DAY 38

PSALM 18:2

"The Lord is my rock, and my fortress, and my deliverer; my God, my strength, in whom will I trust; my buckler, and the horn of my salvation, and my high tower." (KJV)

Dear Father in heaven,

It makes my heart glad just knowing that You included me. Thank You Jesus for dying for me. Holy Spirit thank You for comforting me always. My strength, my rock, my fortress, and my deliverer. My buckler, my high tower, and my avenger! I will forever worship You not because of what You do, but just because You chose me! Father You are Amazing!

"Loving you forever, Lord Jesus and I excitedly wait to sup with you again!"

DAY 39

PSALM 62:8

"Trust in him at all times; ye people, pour out your heart before him; God is a refuge for us. Selah" (KJV)

Dear Father in heaven,

Thank You for being so gracious to us. I thank You for a firm belief in Your reliability, in Your strength, and Your power because You are God, and God alone. Thank You for being my refuge, my shelter from the pursuit of the enemy. Thank You for teaching me how to submit my will to Your will. I will forever pour my heart out to You because only You know the path that I should take. Lord Jesus You are the truth, the way, and the life.

"Loving you forever, Lord Jesus and I excitedly wait to sup with you again!"

DAY 40

1 CORINTHIANS 15:58

"Therefore, my beloved brethren, be ye stedfast, unmoveable, always abounding in the work of the Lord, forasmuch as ye know that your labour is not in vain in the Lord." (KJV)

Dear Father in heaven,

Thank You for the fellowship of the believers. Thank You for our connection to You. Jesus Christ our Lord, the Holy Spirit, and one another. Empower us to remain steadfast; firmly fixed in a place and determined. Dedicated, devoted, loyal, committed, and faithful in the work of the Lord. Abounding and overflowing as the result of knowing that our labour is not in vain in the Lord. Keep us Christ centered, ministry focused, and loving one another as You have loved us.

"Loving you forever, Lord Jesus and I excitedly wait to sup with you again!"

ABOUT THE AUTHOR

Phyllis Welch is a native of Gary, Indiana. She is the mother of one daughter. She graduated from Westside High School and received her formal education at Purdue and Ball State Universities. Upon receiving her Associates Degree and Certification in Medical Administration, she relocated to Jackson, MS.

Elder Welch was blessed to be a graduate of the Full Gospel International Fellowship College of Ordained Elders in June of 2016. She is currently humbly serving at Greater Mt. Zion Church in Columbus, MS, under the Pastoral Leadership of Doran V. Johnson. She faithfully serves as Elder of Protocol, Christian Education, Worship Team Member, and a Teacher for the Y.D.F.C. (Young Disciples for Christ) Youth Ministry.

She is an anointed poet, songwriter, playwright, and author. Her soul purpose is to teach, train, and educate the Body of Christ concerning the principles of the kingdom of God. It is her desire to see all believers mature and become all that God has called them to be in Christ Jesus!